Portsmouth Historic Dockyard

THE HOME OF:

HMS Warrior 1860

HMS Victory

The Mary Rose

The National Museum of the Royal Navy

Action Stations

HMS M.33

Boathouse 4

Royal Marines Museum

Explosion Museum of Naval Firepower

The Royal Navy Submarine Museum

Welcome

For 200 years, Great Britain dominated the seas with a global trading empire stretching from New Zealand in the Southern Ocean to the Hudson Bay on the edge of the Arctic.

From its home at Portsmouth, the Royal Navy commanded this vast enterprise, building some of the most famous warships in the world.

A visit to the Dockyard takes you on a journey through time, allowing you to step onboard historic ships and understand the Royal Navy, past, present and future.

Explore the flagship of Henry VIII's fleet, the Mary Rose; HMS Victory upon which Admiral Nelson defeated the combined French and Spanish fleet at the Battle of Trafalgar; HMS Warrior 1860 the largest iron-hulled armoured warship of Queen Victoria's Black Battle Fleet; the steel-hulled HMS M.33 from World War I and HMS Alliance, a World War II era submarine.

Encounter the people of our past, including King Henry VIII, Admiral Lord Nelson, veterans of the World Wars, as well as the men and women who built and sailed the ships and listen to their compelling stories.

Discover why the ships built and harboured at Portsmouth Historic Dockyard led the way in terms of technology and innovation and how they changed the world.

Embark on the action-packed high seas adventure that is Action Stations; and take a boat tour around Portsmouth Harbour and get close up to the ships of the modern Royal Navy.

Contents

History of Portsmouth Royal Dockyard

Portsmouth Historic Dockyard has a long and distinguished history with Portsmouth Harbour. Its natural shelter was key to defence and trade for Britons, Romans, Saxons and Normans.

The event which most clearly marks the dockyard's rise to national prominence was the construction of the world's first dry dock in 1495, with the first ships built here being launched in 1497. Production in the dry dock continued at pace over the next few years and in 1510 the keel of what was to become the Mary Rose was laid in the dockyard. In 1512 Portsmouth was officially appointed a building centre for the King's ships. No traces of the medieval dockyard remain and the wooden buildings have long been replaced, but the original dry dock lies under the Great Ship Basin, near HMS Victory.

In the 18th century, during a period of almost continuous naval warfare, the dockyard developed into the largest industrial complex in the world. At its centre was the Great Ship Basin, which being tide-free made it easier to service ships, and the Great Stone Dock, the oldest surviving dry dock in the world. Three great storehouses were built between 1760 and 1790, which kept an enormous range of provisions from iron and copper nails, brooms and holystones, to complete sets of rigging. A town within a town, the dockyard boasted fine houses, a church, schools, a mortuary, shops, surgeries and a fire station.

ABOVE: Seamen could choose their mess-mates, a very important right, when time was spent off watch.

The dockyard had been built to service the needs of great sailing ships, but it was poorly prepared for the different requirements of the Victorian steam fleet. As a result, the dockyard was extended northwards into the harbour where a huge new enclosed basin was constructed, along with three new dry docks with engine and boiler factories. In 1848 Queen Victoria opened the new complex, watched by a crowd of 15,000, which soon became the biggest and most modern naval facility in the world. However, within 15 years it had become outdated and further expansion was needed.

The early 20th century saw the building of the great battleship HMS Dreadnought, which was completed in the astonishing time of 366 days. To maintain naval supremacy, Britain constructed a fleet of Dreadnoughts and the dockyard proved it could build battleships cheaper and quicker than any other shipyard worldwide.

This success inevitably meant that the Dockyard was a prime target for bombing by the German air fleet during World War II and suffered severe damage. The post-war years brought a reduction in the naval fleet, but its role was slowly changing and the dockyard was kept busy fitting ships for smaller wars and modernising the fleet to meet the new nuclear and missile age. Following the outbreak of the Falklands War in 1982, the dockyard worked round the clock to load stores, ammunition and fuel and to refit the task force, including the two aircraft carriers, HMS Hermes and HMS Invincible.

Today, Portsmouth Historic Dockyard is situated within a working naval base and has become one of the UK's most popular visitor attractions with many national treasures interspersed with modern naval ships. Throughout its history the dockyard has always been full of energy, industry and innovation and that vibrant culture continues to thrive throughout its historic buildings and the famous ships that are housed here. Today, there is an ongoing programme of current day ships movements which are available for visitors to access.

OPPOSITE: Pre-Dreadnought battleships in line astern in the early 1900s.

Around the Historic Dockyard

Boathouse 4

Boathouse 4 was built in 1939 in response to the need for a rapid rearmament programme prior to the start of World War II. This vast building, incorporating its own dock and locks, is typical of 1930s military industrial architecture.

Boathouse 4 is being restored and will open in 2015 as a Boatbuilding & Heritage Skills Centre. The centre will offer practical, intensive courses in traditional boatbuilding and related skills, and a mezzanine level brasserie with stunning views across Portsmouth Harbour. Visitors will be able to watch traditional boatbuilding in action and enjoy the fascinating story of small boats in the British Navy.

With the restoration of Boathouse 4 you can join and become an apprentice for the day, clocking in at Victory Gate and learning all about the crafts and skills needed. The exhibition gives an insight into the Industrial Revolution in the early 19th century, such as Marc Brunel's block making machines, which allowed the mass production of pulley blocks for ships' rigging and were housed in the Block Mills (see page 51).

The Mast Pond

The Mast Pond was used to store timbers for building and refitting ships, which allowed them to season evenly in the salt water. It was excavated in 1665, initially by Dutch prisoners of war, who were paid one and a half pennies a day, and then by local labour. The Pond is linked to the harbour by a tunnel under the road, which runs through Boathouse 4.

Dockyard Apprentice

In 1911 the great Dreadnought battleships were being constructed at Portsmouth Historic Dockyard. HMS Dreadnought was launched in 1906 and her big guns were so revolutionary that 'dreadnought' became the term for iconic battleships of World War I.

Porter's Lodge and Garden

The Dockyard Porter ensured the smooth running of the site. He guarded the gates, policed the workforce and sold them beer. He lived on site in the Porter's Lodge, which was built in 1708 and is the earliest building in the dockyard.

Within the garden, sculptured seats mirror the hulls of important ships and planting includes herbs used to combat sailors' ailments. The statue of Robert Falcon Scott by his widow, Kathleen Scott, was commissioned after his second expedition to the South Pole ended in his death in 1912.

Historic Boat Workshop

The Historic Boat workshop, originally housed in Boathouse 5, was built as a Mast House with a sail loft in the annex. In the early 19th century there were many buildings of this timber framed construction in the dockyard. Boathouse 5 was built in 1807 and is now home to a unique collection of historic small boats, from whalers to sailing dinghies.

In the Historic Boat Workshop you'll find the *Alexandra Shackleton*, which is a replica of the 22-foot whaler the *James Caird*. It was built to stage a daring re-enactment of Ernest Shackleton's epic 1916 voyage of survival from Elephant Island in Antartica to South Georgia in the South Atlantic after their ship HMS Endurance was crushed by ice.

The Great Ship (No.1) Basin

The vast expanse of water at the top of the main road and beyond HMS Victory is known as The Great Ship Basin or No.1 Basin. Constructed in the late 17th century, the original six dockyards represent one of England's great legacies from the golden age of sail. The sight of the docks and basin filled with ships, similar to HMS Victory, would have been awesome.

The Great Basin was extended through the 1780s and the world's first caisson, or floating dam, was installed at its entrance. Today, HMS Victory occupies Number 2 Dock, The Mary Rose was built over Number 3 Dock, and Number 1 Dock is home to HMS M.33.

Block Mills

Opened in 1803, The Block Mills manufactured the pulley blocks needed for the rigging and gun carriages on ships like HMS Victory. The mills were the world's first steam-powered factory and the block-making machinery was invented by Isambard Kingdom Brunel's father, Marc Brunel. The 45 steam-powered machines were capable of turning out 130,000 pulley blocks in a year.

In their time, the Block Mills were at the cutting edge of the industrial revolution and have been described as the single most important industrial building in the world. At present, they lie within the operational Naval Base and are not open to the public.

Boathouse No.7

This boathouse originally specialised in mast making and building smaller craft for the dockyard, and once accommodated the tallest mast ever built. Today, Boathouse No.7 has been beautifully restored and specialises in fine catering amidst a themed interior. The chef was a submariner and he truly appreciates the fresh, seasonal produce he is now able to work with.

HMS M.33

HMS M.33 is not only the sole remaining British veteran of the bloody Dardanelles Campaign of 1915-1916, but also of the Russian Civil War which followed. The ship is one of just three British warships from World War I still in existence.

HMS M.33 was built in 1915 on the orders of the First Lord of the Admiralty, Winston Churchill. She was a floating gun platform designed to bombard coastal positions from the sea. Her first active operation was the support of the British landings at Suvla during the Battle of Gallipoli in August 1915. She remained stationed at Gallipoli until the evacuation in January 1916. She served in the Mediterranean for the remainder of the War and was involved in the seizure of the Greek fleet at Salamis Bay in 1916.

After the War, *M.33* was sent to Murmansk in Russia to relieve the North Russian Expeditionary Force before returning to Portsmouth to become a mine-laying training ship. She was renamed HMS Minerva.

The National Museum of the Royal Navy and Hampshire County Council have partnered to develop an exciting project to conserve, restore and interpret *M.33* for her centenary in 2015. With Heritage Lottery Fund support this will allow the public onboard for the first time, making HMS M.33 the only warship from World War I open to visitors.

HMS Warrior 1860

HMS Warrior 1860 was the fastest, largest and most powerful warship in the world when she was launched on 29th December 1860. Such was her reputation that enemy fleets were intimidated by her obvious supremacy and deterred from attacking Britain at sea - yet she never fired a shot in anger.

HMS Warrior 1860 was Britain's first iron-hulled, armoured warship and the pride of Queen Victoria's Black Battle Fleet, so called because the iron hulls were all painted black. On her first voyage, *Warrior* caused a sensation; people crowded to see her and she was considered invincible. The combination of iron sides, which offered protection from the new exploding shells, which were first used by Britain and France in the Crimean War, and the ability to carry large guns, changed the nature of marine warfare. She caused a revolution in naval architecture but her combination of steam and sail was out of date within 15 years, by which time there were 22 armour plated battleships in service.

110pdr. gun's crew at drill, supervised by Gunner Colinburn. © J E Wigston.

DON'T MISS

- Start your tour on the upper deck and admire the ship's masts, the Captain's bridge and the propeller well. An operation to raise the 26-tonne propeller, which helped to reduce drag when the ship was powered by sail alone, would involve several hundred of the crew.
- *Warrior's* armoury was impressive. She carried an amazing twenty six 68lb and four 110lb guns enclosed within the armoured citadel of the main gun deck.
- The Captain's quarters are also found on the main deck. They consist of his day cabin, sleeping quarters and a toilet.
- The Wardroom on the lower deck was the mess for the officers. There are 14 cabins off a central dining and relaxation area.
- A visit to the boiler and engine rooms will give you some idea of the demanding and dark conditions faced by the ship's stokers and trimmers who had one of the most vital jobs onboard.

A tour of *Warrior* will give you a clear indication of why the warship earned its formidable reputation. She was built to protect the nation's supremacy at sea following the launch of the first ocean-going iron-clad warship *La Gloire* by the French in 1859. The Royal Navy, under the then First Lord of the Admiralty, Sir John Somerset Pakington, was determined to design a ship that would be regarded as invincible, and would deter France from making a sea assault on Britain. She would have speed, armament and size on her side – in fact, when she was built she was 60% larger than *La Gloire*.

In June 1862 she started active service in the Channel Squadron, patrolling coastal waters and sailing to Lisbon and Gibraltar. Over the next few years her reputation grew and *Warrior* attracted interest at home and overseas. With wooden ships now a thing of the past, there was a desire worldwide to design and build ships with thicker armour, more powerful guns and efficient engines.

It's ironic that having become the ultimate deterrent against attack, *Warrior's* life as a warship was short-lived. She was soon replaced by faster designs, with bigger guns and even thicker armour, and in 1871 was downgraded to coastguard and reserve services.

A few years later, it was decided that her rotten fore and main masts were not worth the cost of repair, and *Warrior* was placed in the reserve. She was converted to a floating school for the Navy and re-named *Vernon III* in 1904.

Despite her awesome reputation the unthinkable happened – she was put up for sale as scrap in 1924. But no buyer could be found, and five years later she was converted into a floating oil pontoon at Pembroke Dock and renamed again – this time as *Oil Fuel Hulk C77*.

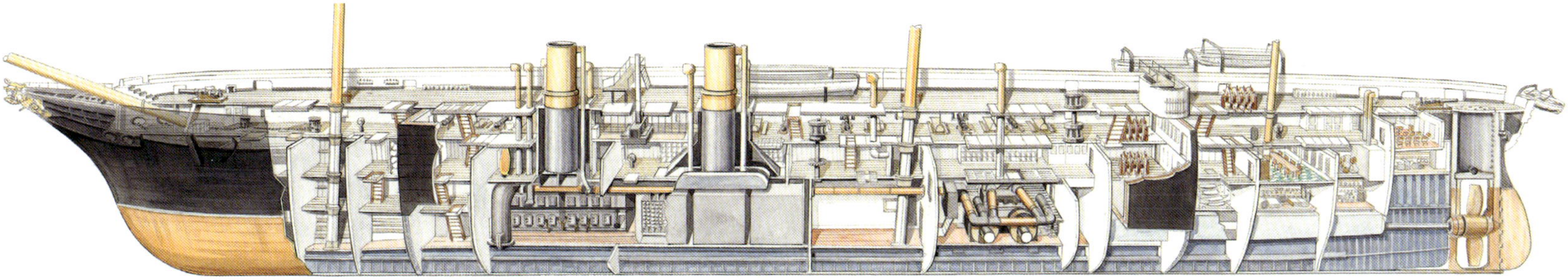

There were more fears for *Warrior's* future when the oil depot closed in 1978, but thankfully the Manifold Trust, formed by Sir John Smith and launched to restore threatened items of national heritage, stepped in to save the only surviving member of Queen Victoria's renowned Black Battle Fleet. With the cost of her restoration being underwritten by the Trust, *Warrior* was passed on to the Maritime Trust a year later.

Warrior was towed 800 miles to Hartlepool where the world's largest maritime project ever undertaken began. In 1983, ownership was transferred to the Ship's Preservation Trust, which became known as the Warrior Preservation Trust in 1985. Considerable research was needed to establish exactly what the ship had been like, but using information from a remarkable journal of a 14-year-old sailor, dated 1861 and discovered by the National Museum of the Royal Navy, the restoration could begin.

After eight years of skillful rebuilding, on the afternoon of Friday 12th June 1987, *Warrior* was pulled by tugs from her moorings to begin the four-day journey back to Portsmouth, a flotilla of tankers, ferries and trawlers turned out all along the east coast to salute her.

Who knows what would have happened to *Warrior* if the Manifold Trust hadn't stepped in to save her in 1978. Thankfully, the painstaking restoration has proved to be a major success, providing a valuable insight into what life was like onboard an elite warship from the Victorian era.

FACT FILE

- Napoleon III of France described *Warrior* as "*a black snake amongst rabbits*", such was the warship's supremacy of the seas.
- *Warrior* was the largest warship of her day at 9,210 tons displacement.
- The ship's top speed under steam was 14.3 knots, with sails it was 13 knots.
- *Warrior's* first captain was the Hon Arthur Cochrane, a brave seaman and born leader, who had a flair for technical matters.
- It took up to 176 men four to five hours to raise each of *Warrior's* 5.6-tonne anchors.
- In the boiler and engine rooms, *Warrior's* stokers would spend hours each day shovelling coal and ash by hand in temperatures that could reach over 100 degrees Fahrenheit (37.8 degrees Celsius).

Harbour Tours and Waterbus

The history of the British Navy at Portsmouth dates back 1,200 years to its earliest days under King Alfred the Great in the 860s. This wide natural inlet in the coastline is a flooded river valley protected by a deep narrow entrance on two sides of the dockyard, here and at Gosport, which makes an ideal natural harbour.

Roman and Saxon strongholds were constructed on the northern shore to defend against Viking attacks and to protect trade, but the harbour's first permanent fort, Portchester Castle, was built after the Norman conquest in 1066.

Portsea Island, at the entrance to the harbour, was used as a mustering station for armies during the wars with France, and by the late 12th century a small town had grown on the south-western corner of the Island to accommodate workers and to service troops. In 1194 King Richard I granted this town, known as Portsmouth, a Royal Charter to construct a dockyard, and in 1212 King John protected the new dockyard with a great wall.

On the Harbour Tour you will see many of the fortifications that were built to protect Portsmouth over the centuries, in particular the Round Tower at the harbour entrance and the Solent forts which formed the centre of a string of fortifications along the coast during the Napoleonic Wars.

Portsmouth is still the home of the modern Royal Navy and taking the Harbour Tour is the best way to appreciate the size and scale of its impressive fleet of ships. The tour offers unrivalled views of Britain's modern frigates, destroyers and helicopter carriers, as well as historic buildings and the dramatic skyline.

FACT FILE

- HMS Alliance was launched in 1945, just as World War II came to an end.
- She became one of the submarines used during the Cold War between NATO and the Soviet Union.
- She was decommissioned in 1973 and became a static training boat until August 1979 at HMS Dolphin, replacing HMS Tabard.
- In April 2014, *Alliance's* £7million conservation project was completed.
- HMS Alliance is a Royal Navy A-class – Amphion class or Acheron class submarine.
- *Alliance's* range was 15,000 miles.

HMS Alliance

At the Royal Navy Submarine Museum

HMS Alliance is Britain's only remaining World War II submarine and stands as a memorial to the 5,300 British submariners who have lost their lives in service.

At the start of World War II, the Royal Navy had 100 submarines similar to HMS Alliance, although *Alliance* wasn't launched until near the end of the conflict in 1945. She was one of 14 A-class long range submarines built for service in the Far East, patrolling the vast areas of the Pacific Ocean.

In 1958 HMS Alliance was modified for Cold War duties where her main purpose became hunting enemy submarines, so she had to become faster and quieter when underwater. As a result, her low conning tower and anti-aircraft guns were replaced with a fin that completely covered her periscopes when she dived. These alterations made *Alliance* more streamlined and better equipped for submarine warfare in the Cold War era.

During active service, *Alliance* was home to over 65 officers and men and could remain submerged for up to 36 hours. She was one of only seven boats fitted with a snort mast – a submarine snorkel which allowed her to remain submerged while taking in air from the surface.

A tour of *Alliance* begins in the forward torpedo store, then on through the accommodation space to the control room, where experienced submariner guides demonstrate the navigation systems including diving and surfacing. The tour continues through the galley and on to the heart of the submarine, the engine room, before culminating in the aft torpedo compartment, where the guides explain how submariners would escape in an emergency. Along the way, you can also peer through the working periscopes to view Portsmouth Harbour.

Alliance forms the centrepiece of the Royal Navy Submarine Museum and along with *Holland I* (Britain's first submarine) and *X24* (the only surviving midget submarine from World War II), represents the core of the museum's unique collection, which also contains thousands of photographs, documents, ship plans and artefacts.

The Royal Navy Submarine Museum is located in Gosport on the former site of HMS Dolphin; home to the Submarine Service for 100 years. A complimentary waterbus takes visitors across the harbour from Portsmouth Historic Dockyard.

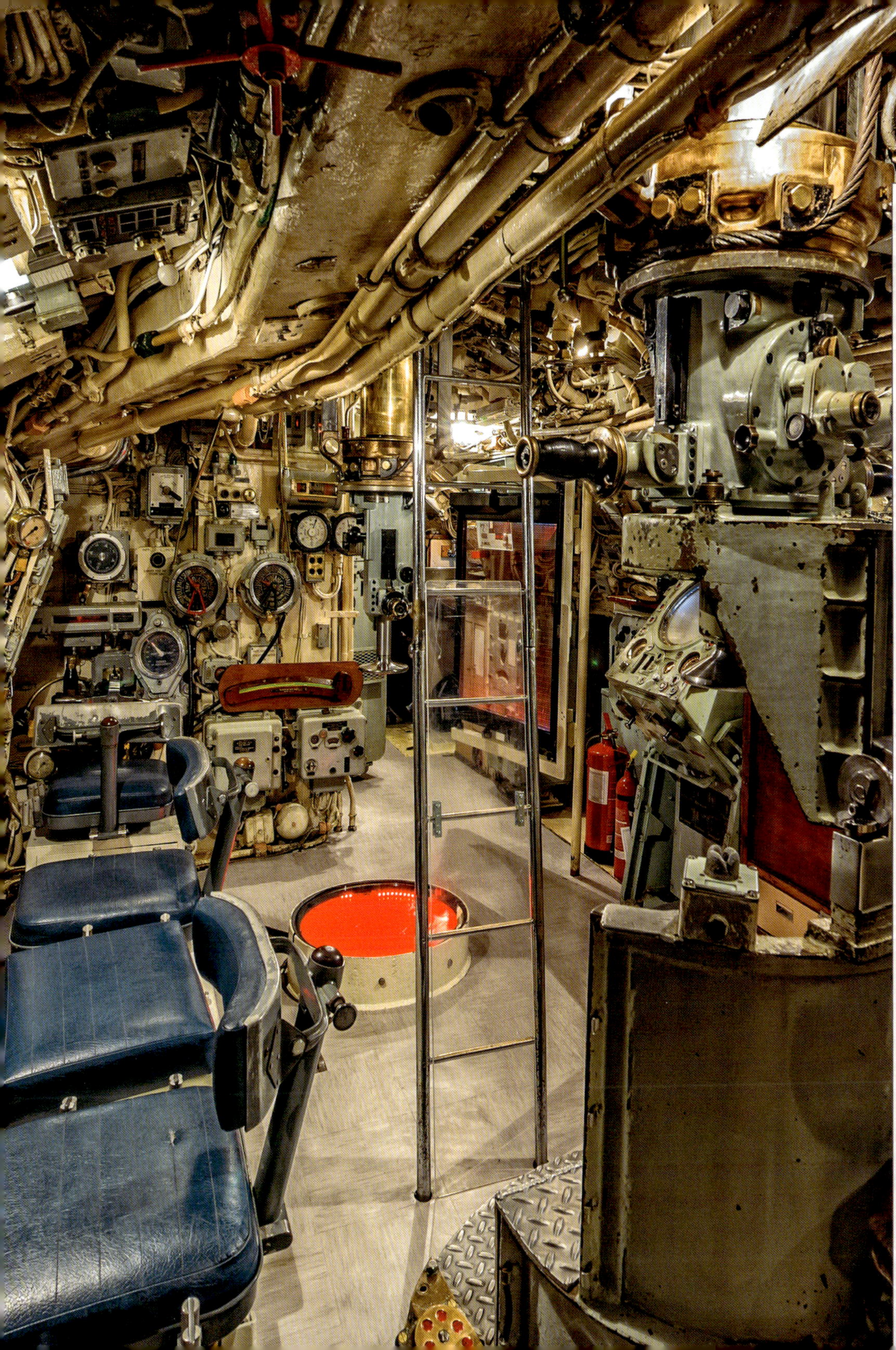

DON'T MISS AT THE ROYAL NAVY SUBMARINE MUSEUM

- The first known Royal Navy submarine flag - a small military silk that was produced by Geoffrey Phillips Ltd in 1915 to be given away in a cigarette packet. It shows a miniature version of an early submarine flag.

- The main search periscope from HMS E11, which was commissioned in 1914. The top section of the periscope was pierced by a Turkish shell during her first patrol in the Sea of Marmara, in May 1915.

- A totem pole was the mascot of HMS Totem. It was made to replace the original which was stolen sometime in the 1950s whilst on a visit to Halifax, Canada. There was a legend amongst the crew that if the submarine went to sea without the totem pole, disaster would ensue.

- The Uckers Cup, presented to Stoker F Evans of HMS Taku in 1944 for winning an Uckers competition. It is made out of an old 'Ideal' milk tin mounted on a stem of a nut and bolt. Uckers is a traditional naval game and is an advanced form of Ludo.

- The first ever locomotive torpedo, designed in 1866 by Robert Whitehead. The torpedo is named after the torpedo fish, which is an electric ray that attacks by delivering a stunning shock to its prey.

DON'T MISS

- '*All of One Company*' in the HMS Gallery. This powerful film brings you face to face with the drama and dangers of fighting at sea, in the words of those who went to war.
- The interactive timeline in the HMS Gallery, with photographs, documents and film from the last 100 years of history.
- William Wyllie's amazing 42-feet long oil painting, '*The Panorama of the Battle of Trafalgar*', at the Trafalgar Experience in the Victory Gallery.
- '*Spirit of the Figurehead*' display, in the Victory Gallery. Walk among the carved giants in the Museum's collection of ship figureheads from the late 18th century.
- The personal items belonging to Admiral Horatio Nelson, in the Nelson Gallery. Look out for the letter he wrote days after the amputation of his right arm.

National Museum of the Royal Navy Portsmouth

The Royal Navy has helped to shape the world. It made Britain a dominant sea power, protected its trade in troubled times and defended Britain from invasion or carried the attack overseas. The Royal Navy has touched the lives of millions of people worldwide, affected servicemen and women and the families of those who built, serviced and supplied its ships and influenced the lives of communities overseas.

The National Museum of the Royal Navy Portsmouth brings this history to life. It showcases treasures from the past 350 years and examines the common threads which link the sailor of England's 'Wooden Walls' to the professional modern crews. Today, the Royal Navy has changed its size, its role in the world, its friends and its enemies.

Technology has revolutionised ships and the lives of those onboard. However, ships still sail, families are still left behind and crews still face the challenges of life at sea.

The museum's major gallery **HMS – Hear My Story** opened in 2014 and tells the undiscovered stories from the ordinary men and women of the ships which have shaped the Navy's amazing history over the last 100 years, the century of greatest change. **HMS** brings you closer than ever before to the real Royal Navy. Cutting edge interpretation lets you see and hear the stories of the Navy in war and during peacetime; from the storms of the Arctic to the heat of Afghanistan. Immersive technology lets you disguise your own ship, hunt a submarine and send messages in code. Meet the veterans who can tell you first hand their stories of living and fighting at sea. This is an exhibition where your story matters. You can take part, share precious personal memories about yourself or your family, add these stories to history and join the debate on what the future may hold. **HMS** has a dramatic and moving story to tell. Come face to face with the people of the Royal Navy through their stories and share in their triumphs and disasters.

Right next door, the museum's exhibitions focus on the 18th and early 19th centuries. **The Sailing Navy** shows the realities of fighting at sea in the age of sail. **Nelson: the Hero and the Man** examines Nelson's colourful, crowded and short life. He master-minded some of British history's most resounding victories – at the Nile in 1798, Copenhagen in 1801 and Trafalgar in 1805 – losing an arm, the sight in one eye, and ultimately, his life.

Nelson had a tempestuous and very public love affair with Emma Hamilton, one of the most beautiful women of his day. He was affectionate, engaging, a devoted friend and father, but at times ruthless and occasionally even cruel. Uninspiring and less than heroic in his personal appearance, he was also one of Britain's most charismatic leaders, able to inspire devotion, even love, in those who served with him.

The Sir Donald Gosling Victory Gallery explores the history of Britain's most famous warship from the laying of her keel to her significant battles. Here visitors can walk through the multi-media show the 'Trafalgar Experience', meeting Nelson and his great foe Napoleon, feeling the blast on the main gun deck during the Battle. This gallery will evolve in future years to look at the story of *Victory's* survival after Trafalgar, and the efforts it took to preserve her.

FACT FILE

- The Navy's rum ration was first introduced for crews in the West Indies in 1740. It was only abolished on 'Black Tot Day' in July 1970.
- Nelson joined the Navy when he was 12 years old; by 15 he had already travelled to the Arctic, the West Indies and India.
- On the eve of World War I, 25% of the budget the central government spent was used for the Royal Navy.
- During World War II, the Royal Navy had over 790,000 men and women serving at its peak in 1944.
- Did you know the Navy has its own language called 'Jack Speak'? A 'banana bedstead' is a hammock and 'angry palm tree' is actually a helicopter.

As HMS Victory undergoes her most extensive refit since Trafalgar, the exhibitions will share the forensic analysis changing our understanding of *Victory's* past and the scientific investigations showing new ways of securing her future.

Make sure you visit the latest display in the museum's new special exhibition gallery; **HMS Hear My Story**, where you can explore in more detail key events of the great war at sea between 1914-18. In 2014 the exhibition **Racing to War: the Royal Navy and 1914** commemorates the centenary of World War I, telling the story of the opening months of war at sea and last years of peace. Future exhibitions will explore in more detail key events of **The Great War at Sea**.

HMS Victory

There have been many celebrated warships in Britain's naval history but HMS Victory can justifiably claim to be the most famous of them all. Having served as Vice-Admiral Lord Nelson's flagship at the Battle of Trafalgar, she has become one of the UK's most cherished visitor attractions.

The death of Nelson onboard *Victory* during the Battle of Trafalgar is an iconic moment in history, and one of the main reasons millions of people visit the warship. The Vice-Admiral was fatally shot on October 21, 1805 by a French sailor in the mizzen mast of *La Redoubtable*. The spot on the quarter deck where Nelson fell is marked by a brass plaque.

ABOVE: Victory sailed into battle at a walking pace, facing the full force of enemy guns.

ABOVE: The brass plaque to mark where Nelson fell on the quarter deck.

After being shot, Nelson was carried to the orlop deck, where many other injured seamen and officers were awaiting medical attention from surgeon William Beatty. Beatty feared the worst as he examined Nelson, finding that the musket ball had penetrated deep into his chest and broken his spine – three hours later Nelson was dead.

Victory suffered the highest casualties of the British ships at Trafalgar, 51 of the servicemen onboard were killed, 11 died of their wounds and 91 were wounded and survived.

Victory had experienced quite a number of year's service before her most famous role as Nelson's flagship at the Battle of Trafalgar. In fact, Nelson was less than a year old when her keel was laid at Chatham Dockyard in 1759. It was the '*Annus Mirabilis*', or 'Year of Victories', for Britain and it is believed that the ship's name may have been chosen to commemorate this occasion. However, people had misgivings about calling her *Victory* as a previous ship of the same name had been wrecked with the loss of all hands.

FACT FILE

- It took a lot of timber to build *Victory* – around 6,000 trees were felled for the cause.
- *Victory* carried 6,510 square yards (5,440 square metres) of sail and had a maximum speed of 10 knots (11.5 miles per hour).
- She was designed to carry 100 guns, although her armament varied between 98 and 104 guns.
- When fully armed, *Victory* displaced 3,500 tons.
- She once stayed at sea for two years and three months without entering port.
- *Victory* was saved for the nation in 1922, and placed into dry dock where she remains today. She is the oldest commissioned warship in the world.
- In 2009, *Victory* celebrated the 250th anniversary of the laying of her keel.
- *Victory* remains a commissioned warship of the Royal Navy, with a commanding officer and crew.

DON'T MISS

- The brass plaque on the Quarter Deck where Lord Nelson was shot. After being wounded, Nelson was carried to the orlop deck where he died three hours later.
- *Victory's* Brodie stove in the galley. Every member of the 821-man crew ate food that had been cooked on this single, surprisingly small stove.
- *Victory's* broadside of guns. At the Battle of Trafalgar the ship carried 104 guns, each weighing around three tonnes, spread over four decks – eight of the original guns are still onboard *Victory* today.
- The Admiral's Office in the day cabin, where he planned battle strategy, commanded the fleet and wrote his dispatches. It was at the breakfast table here that Nelson wrote his famous prayer before the Battle of Trafalgar.
- The Quarter Deck, where Nelson surveyed the enemy fleet.

HMS Victory was floated out in 1765 and stayed afloat in reserve at Chatham Dockyard for 13 years. *Victory* left Chatham to begin life as one of the most successful naval ships of all time, leading fleets in a series of history-changing wars including the American War of Independence and the Napoleonic War.

However *Victory* achieved her lasting fame at the Battle of Trafalgar, despite being 40 years old. Even after her finest hour she went on to further service in the Baltic and other seas before her career as a fighting ship ended in 1812. Coincidentally, she was 47 years old, the same age Nelson had been when he died.

ABOVE: Seamen slept, ate and socialised between the guns.

Victory was saved for posterity in 1922 following a national appeal, and placed into dry dock at Portsmouth Historic Dockyard where she remains today.

Visitors to Portsmouth Historic Dockyard can now trace the development of Britain's naval advancements. *Victory* is located between the 16th century Tudor warship the Mary Rose, the Victorian-built iron-hulled, armoured warship HMS Warrior 1860 and the steel built HMS M.33 of the early 20th century.

Victory is now owned and presented to visitors by the National Museum of the Royal Navy, having had her custodianship transferred from the Ministry of Defence in March 2012.

The Mary Rose

OPPOSITE: The Mary Rose by Geoff Hunt.

Step back in time and explore Henry VIII's favourite warship – raised from the depths of the Solent and painstakingly preserved for future generations. The Mary Rose is the only 16th century warship on display anywhere in the world, and the new award-winning museum reunites her with many of her artefacts and crew, capturing the moment in time when she sank 470 years ago.

The story of the Mary Rose is one of the most fascinating in naval history. A tale of battles fought against the French for over 30 years before sinking off the coast of Portsmouth in 1545. It's an account of her being raised from the seabed more than 400 years later, and of her meticulous restoration.

The ship captured the world's imagination when she was raised from the Solent in 1982, and her dramatic story is now revealed in full and graphic style inside the purpose-built, £27million Mary Rose Museum, which opened its doors to visitors in May 2013.

Inside the museum the starboard half of the ship is housed in a 'hot box', enabling it to dry out gently over the next few years. The impressive vessel is truly captivating and can be viewed on several levels through viewing windows.

In addition to the ship, the collection of artefacts is just as impressive. Over 19,000 artefacts were discovered during the excavation, including personal belongings such as wooden bowls, leather shoes, musical instruments and nit combs, and many of the ship's weapons, from longbows to two-tonne guns. There is even a well-preserved skeleton of the dog 'Hatch', the onboard 'ratter' and unofficial ship's mascot. The museum offers a unique insight into the life of crew members too, with forensic science used to bring the story of the Mary Rose to life.

FACT FILE

- Before sinking, the Mary Rose saw 34 years of service as Henry VIII's flagship.
- The Mary Rose sank in 1545 and was raised from the seabed in 1982.
- Almost 19,000 artefacts have been recovered from the wreck site. They all have to be kept within environmentally controlled conditions to prevent disintegration.
- The final recorded crew list contained 185 soldiers, 200 mariners and 30 gunners, this is in addition to officers and their staff. Only 25-30 men survived the sinking.
- The search for, and discovery of, the Mary Rose was a result of the dedication of one man, the late Alexander McKee. In 1965 he initiated '*Project Solent Ships*' to investigate wrecks in the Solent. His real hope was to find the Mary Rose.
- Excavation work took 12 man-years on the seabed, involving 28,000 dives between 1979 and 1982.
- 60 million people worldwide watched the raising of the hull live on TV.

CRAFTSMANSHIP
IN WOOD

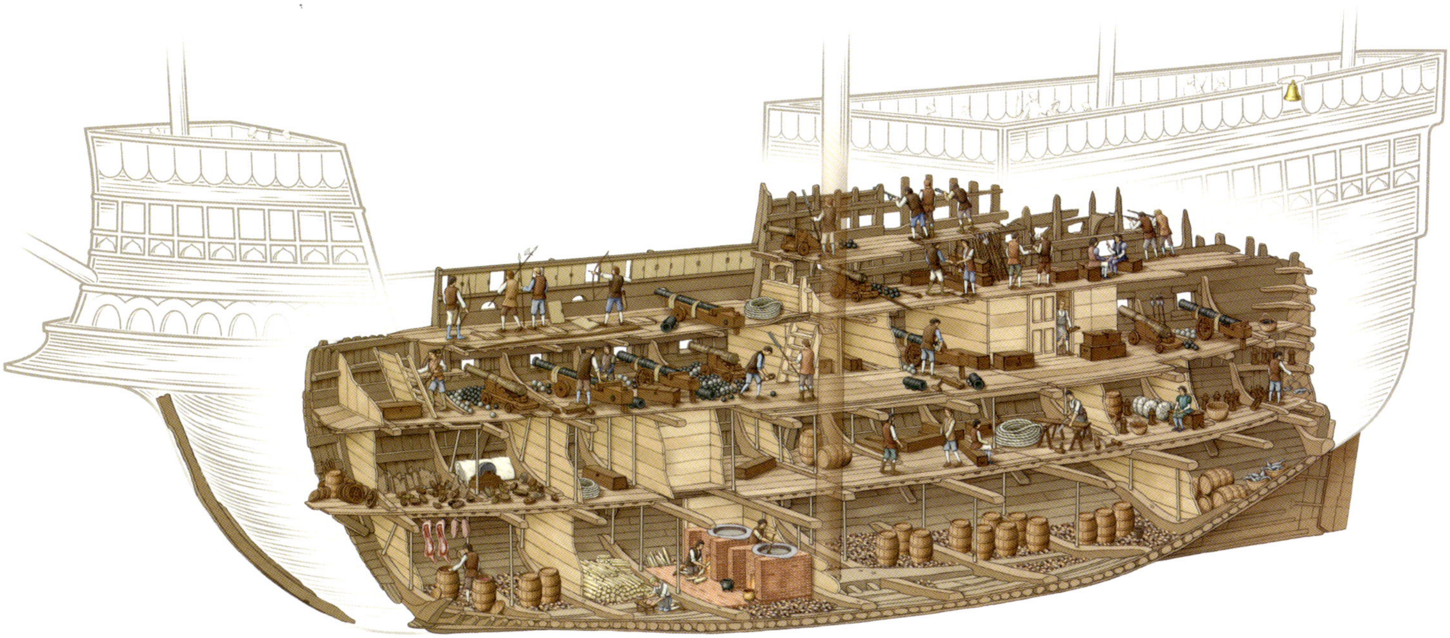

When the Mary Rose capsized and sank off the coast of Portsmouth on 19th July 1545, during the Battle of The Solent, it looked like she was lost forever, along with most of the 500 men onboard. Despite strenuous attempts to salvage the ship, she remained stuck on the seabed and by the end of the year all efforts had been abandoned.

It took more than 400 years to finally rediscover the Mary Rose and start the complicated and delicate task of salvaging her. For centuries Mary Rose lay on her starboard side, leaving the port side exposed to the Solent currents and marine organisms. However, over time the site was covered with a layer of silt, which fortunately sealed it off and protected the ship from further erosion.

The Mary Rose was rediscovered using modern sonar equipment. Archaeologists and volunteer divers excavated every cubic centimetre of the ship, using their hands and small trowels to uncover precious artefacts. It was a long and arduous process but the moment the world had been waiting for arrived in 1982, when she was raised from the depths of the seabed for the first time in 437 years.

After the hull was salvaged and towed triumphantly home into Portsmouth Historic Dockyard, the difficult task of preserving the ancient water-logged timbers began. Since 1994, the ship has been sprayed with a water-soluble wax (polyethylene glycol) which penetrated the wood to preserve it for all time. The sprays have now been switched off and the timbers will be carefully dried until 2016, completing the 34-year preservation project.

There is so much to learn about the Mary Rose; from how she was born out of Henry VIII's need to build up his fleet to combat the threat of strong French and Spanish navies, to whether she was named after Mary Tudor, Henry VIII's sister, or the Virgin Mary who was also known at the time as 'The Mystic Rose'. The Mary Rose helps you delve into the ship's past and discover the answers.

DON'T MISS

- The surviving starboard half of the ship (which is colossal, even by today's standards) is still sealed off, though dazzlingly visible through viewing windows. For the best view of the ship a ride in the panoramic viewing lift is recommended.
- 'Hatch', one of the more famous exhibits in the Mary Rose, and popular with all ages. He was the ratter onboard. Recent developments in DNA analysis have found him to be most closely related to modern Jack Russell Terriers.
- The historic story of the sinking of the Mary Rose, which occupies a wall of the exhibition in the form of a digitally enhanced image of a painting of the Battle of The Solent.
- The ship's objects which are located opposite the remains of the hull. These guns, carriages and equipment are arranged as they would have been onboard minutes before she sank.
- Finding out what life would have been like for the crew of the Mary Rose, including individuals such as the ship's surgeon and master carpenter. Their stories are brought to life alongside the tools of their trades.

FACT FILE

- *"I have spent a number of years in the Navy but I have never had so much fun in 20 minutes!"* said HRH the Duke of York on opening Action Stations in 2001.
- The indoor climbing frame is one of the largest in Europe at 8.4 metres (over 27 feet), and was built in Houston, Texas.
- Boathouse 6 was built in 1845 and was in use until the Portsmouth Blitz in March 1941, when a bomb destroyed much of the building.
- Boathouse 6 was one of the earliest buildings constructed with a metal frame to support boat storage on the upper floors.
- The Type-23 frigate featured in *'Command Approved'* was also a star in the 1997 James Bond adventure *'Tomorrow Never Dies'* with Pierce Brosnan.
- 13 Type-23 frigates are in service with the Royal Navy today.

Action Stations

Action Stations is a high-tech, interactive indoor attraction housed in Boathouse 6. The boathouse itself was built between 1845 and 1848, and like the technology it now features inside, it was once at the forefront of design and innovation in the Victorian era.

Its primary purpose was to repair and maintain small craft known as 'ship's boats'. These small vessels serviced the larger ships in the fleet, such as HMS Victory, which at the time were too large to enter the dockyard and had to anchor in the Solent, at Spithead.

Hundreds of ship's boats were needed to ferry sailors to and from the dockyard and to load and unload supplies and cargo.

Boathouse 6 was the largest maintenance building of its kind, and the three huge doors used to enter Action Stations today allowed these small boats to be hauled up the slipway from the mast pond and through the doors, before being hoisted to the first floor for repairs.

The building took direct hits to the first and second floors during World War II, and was roughly patched up by the Royal Navy. However its usefulness had diminished and it was no longer needed by the Navy. Work began in 1998 to turn Boathouse 6 into the state-of-the-art attraction we see today.

Action Stations was officially opened by the Duke of York in 2001, and features a unique series of physical challenges, simulators and technological experiments, which put visitors at the heart of the modern naval experience.

Royal Marines Museum

At the Royal Marines Museum, housed in the historic Victorian barracks at Eastney, you will take a journey through 350 years of naval history. The Royal Marines are the Royal Navy's elite fighting force, founded by Charles II in 1664 and have been at the forefront of conflicts, including the Battle of Trafalgar, both World Wars, the Falklands War and the recent conflicts in Iraq and Afghanistan.

The museum houses a collection of paintings of naval heroes, battles and battleships, marine mascots and over 8,000 medals including ten Victoria Crosses. There are also personal stories, such as that of Hannah Snell, who ran away to sea in 1745, joined the Marines as a man, was wounded and received her pension as a woman.

This family-friendly museum has hands-on interactive games, simulators, sight, sound and touch experiences. Follow a Commando recruit through training and on to deployment around the world, creep through the jungle and meet a snake called 'Bill', take a trip down memory lane in the World War II home-front kitchen or experience World War I trench warfare on the western front.

Finish your visit by climbing onboard the rigid raider and assault course and enjoy lunch in the award-winning Quartermaster's Kitchen.

Explosion Museum of Naval Firepower

The story of naval warfare is told in dramatic style at Explosion, an interactive museum housed in the Royal Navy's former Ordnance Depot, at Priddy's Hard, centred around The Grand Magazine, a listed powder magazine from 1771.

Priddy's Hard was far enough from the main dockyard for the safe storage of up to 6,500 barrels of gunpowder. In the Napoleonic Wars, this was where all Royal Navy warships including HMS Victory came to load up their guns and ammunition, collecting them from small boats called 'powder hoys' which had in turn collected barrels of gunpowder carried in barrows down the Rolling Way to the harbour edge.

The site has adapted as times have changed. With the introduction of breech loading guns in the late 1850s, it was no longer necessary to make barrels or test gunpowder here and a series of large magazines were built to fill and store shells. In the 1880s, the substitution of highly explosive cordite for gunpowder as a propellant required the building of a narrow gauge railway to transport ordnance between filling and storage buildings. Change continued through the 20th century with the development of torpedoes, depth charges and small arms up to the arrival of guided missiles in the 1960s. The last time Priddy's Hard supplied weapons to the Royal Navy was during the Falklands War in 1982.